Ephemeral Splendor

By

J.J.BHATT

ISBN:

9798366915786

Title:

Ephemeral Splendor

Author:

J.J. Bhatt

Published and Distributed by Amazon and Kindle worldwide.

This book is manufactured in the Unites States of America.

Recent Books by J.J. Bhatt
(Available from Amazon)

HUMAN ENDEAVOR: *Essence & Mission/ A Call for Global Awakening,* *(2011)*

ROLLING SPIRITS: *Being Becoming /*A Trilogy, (2012)

ODYSSEY OF THE DAMNED: *A Revolving Destiny,* (2013).

PARISHRAM: *Journey of the Human Spirits,* (2014).

TRIUMPH OF THE BOLD: *A Poetic Reality,* (2015).

THEATER OF WISDOM, *(2016).*

MAGNIFICENT QUEST: *Life, Death & Eternity,* (2016).

ESSENCE OF INDIA: *A Comprehensive Perspective,* (2016).

ESSENCE OF CHINA: *Challenges & Possibilities,* (2016).

BEING & MORAL PERSUASION: *A Bolt of Inspiration,* (2017).

REFELCTIONS, RECOLLECTIONS & EXPRESSIONS, (2018).

ONE, TWO, THREE... ETERNITY: *A Poetic Odyssey,* (2018).

INDIA: *Journey of Enlightenment,* (2019a).

SPINNING MIND, SPINNING TIME: *C'est la vie,* (2019b).Book 1.

MEDITATION ON HOLY TRINITY, *(2019c), Book 2.*

ENLIGHTENMENT: *Fiat l,* (2019d), Book 3.

BEING IN THE CONTEXTUAL ORBIT: *Rhythm, Melody & Meaning,* (2019e).

QUINTESSENCE: *Thought & Action,* (2019f).

THE WILL TO ASCENT: *Power of Boldness & Genius,* (2019g).

RIDE ON A SPINNING WHEEL: *Existence Introspected,* (2020a).

A FLASH OF LIGHT: *Splendors, Perplexities & Riddles,* (2020b).

ON A ZIG ZAG TRAIL: *The Flow of Life,* (2020c).

UNBOUNDED: *An Inner Sense of Destiny* (2020d).

REVERBERATIONS: The *Cosmic Pulse,* (2020e).

LIGHT & DARK: *Dialogue and Meaning,* (2021a).

ROLLING REALITY: *Being in flux,* (2021b).

FORMAL SPLENDOR: *The Inner Rigor,* (2021c).

TEMPORAL TO ETERNAL: *Unknown Expedition,* (2021d).

TRAILBLAZERS: *Spears of Courage,* (2021e).

TRIALS & ERRORS: *A Path to Human Understanding,* (2021f).

MEASURE OF HUMAN EXPERIENCE: *Brief Notes,* (2021g).

LIFE: *An Ellipsis (2022a).*

VALIDATION: *The Inner Realm of Essence* (2022b).

LET'S ROLL: *Brave Heart,* (2022c).

BEING BECOMING, (2022d).

INVINCIBLE ,(2022e).

 THE CODE: *DESTINY,* **(2022f).**

LIFE DIMYSTIFIED, (2022g).

 ESSENTIAL HUMANITY,(2022h).

 MORAL ADVENTURE, (2022i) .

SPIRALING SPHERES (2022h).

EPHEMERAL SPLENDOR, (2023a).

CHAOTIC HARMONY, (2023b).

PREFACE

Ephemeral Splendor exclusively focuses on the modern human being who is struggling to unfold the right path to roll, especially when his life is brief and the journey ever so long; perhaps, cyclically endless!

While on the highway of trials and errors, he faces myriad challenges including his very state of anxiety, fear and confusion in the fast changing world. Only way out for him is to relearn, " how to purify his corrupt mind," and be a stubborn will to take a giant leap forward with full self-confidence, no matter whatever may be the risk, but without the loss of truth, *salva veritatis.*

J.J. Bhatt

CONTENTS

Spark

Life so well
Illuminated with
All the wonders,
Creativity and
Boldness

Let human
Keep dancing
With joy, hope
And harmony
And be grateful

Let life be
Sparked by every
Discovery, every
Endeavor and every
Rewarding dream

Life,
What a
Precious pearl
Driven by myriad
Ambitions

Let it
Roll from
Temporal to eternal
With all its wonders,
Creativity and boldness
Soul to soul…

Invitation

Come,
Let us begin
Journey on
Anew path,

I mean,
Far from
Lies,
Deceptions
And disorder

Let us
Absorb
All that is good
Via our intuitive
Thoughts

Let us
Transcend the
Empirical realm and
Land into the reality
Called, "Deep Silence"
Where we may have
A chance!

Trapeze

So the drama
Flows, "Subjective
Being lost into the
World of objective
Truth"

Its, being
Hanging on a
Thin wire and like
A trapeze fighting
To balance the
Meaning at
Every sec

On the way,
Light goes off now
And then and his
Mind is
Distracted time and
Again

Spectators
Keep cheering
To keep him walking
And finish the brave act

If he is
Calm, he would be
The hero, if not,
He would be
A fat, "Zero!"

Gauntlet

Hello
Young braves,
Why not be the
Constant courage
And inspiration
While you got
The chance

I say,
Why not bring
Your critical point
Of view upfront
And be the constructive
Force of the time

Why wait
For others while
You can deliver the
Viable blueprint

Just drop
All the evil habits
Of the elders and
Stake
Out your claim,
"To build a better world
By conquering the mind
It self"

Young braves,
This is your time.
This is your challenge.
And this is your destiny,
Waiting…

.

Spinning
Soul

The first cause
Seems a rational
Adventure alright

Wonder what
Is the final cause
To justify human
Essence in this
Turbulent time!

In-between is
That journey of the
Human spirit, but his
Direction not so well
Defined

He's still
Twisting into the
Uncertainty and
Thick greed and the
End seems too far

He's burdened
By more queries than
Answers to his sincere
Endeavors and the end
Seems too far...

Mighty
Gift

What a
Unique gift is
This human;
Possessing the
"Moral Self"

He is
A fearless
Freewill and
Can walk
Million miles to
Know his truth

Indeed,
What a genius is
This human who
Can bring forth,
Harmony and hope

He is
A sincere being
Ready to lift the
World through
The power of his
Determined will...

Love!

If we had
Understood,
"What is love
All about"

We wouldn't
Have to suffer
Through for a
Long

We kept
Drowning not
In love, but in
Mistrust;
Tearing apart
Sweet dream

Love,
What a
Beautiful gif'
That we never
Understood

Love
What an
Eternal joy
To be that
We ignored
It all the way…

Consequence

This desk
Full of dozen
Pens and pencils,
Scissors, tapes,
Eraser and spider
Web of electronics

All ready
In dressing up
My floating
Thoughts into
Written notions
Before the world
Of opinion only

Many shall
Criticize 'em, a few
May welcome 'em and
Most wouldn't give
A damn, whatever
Worth it may be

Well
That is the
Fate of being in
"Ephemeral Splendor"
Where "I am so
Brief in life simply..."

New
Dawn

Is it not
Time,
Big nations
Awakens to
Their respective
Conscience

Is it
Too late to
Look out,
"Humanity be
Above all"

Is it not
A necessity to
Own, "Global
Peace" with deep
Understanding

Let the
"World Mind"
Begin to walk
Forward,
In the name of
Children's dream

Big
Mirror

If this
Journey turns
Into an ever
Inspiring good,
There is no need to
Get off the track

If this
Trail is full of
Strengthening
Our wills

There is
No hurry
To get off the
Set game

Keep
Eye on the
Clock and keep
The image steady
While looking at the
Grand mirror,
Forever …

Great
Ride

We
Keep
Alive with
Possibilities

Let the
Universal
Connectivity
Of the souls
Catch-up in
Time

Let
The core
Essence of
Our births be
The truth-giver,
All the way
To the end....

Nemesis

Wonder,
What is the
Self-evident
Necessity
Of our kind

Why
We're
Helplessly
Immersed in this
Crazy hedonism and
Ignoring the moral
Self

Aren't we
Losing
Something
Called,

"Dignity,
Freedom and
Humanity in this
Overwhelming
Techno milieu, or
What!"

Illuminators

All we're
Is the ever
Expanding
Consciousness

I mean,
We're the
Arrow of mind
In flight from
Temporal to be
Eternal

While
En route,
We're the
Thunders of
New ideas and
"Self-realization"
At the core

Why
Not then be
Illuminating
Spirits and

Let
Us be in the
Lapse of
Cosmic radiance
And be the inspired
Wills....

That's it

We've been
Spinning,
Through
Birth to death
And birth again!

Humanity
Just another
Manifest born
In it and million
Miles to go

Paradoxically,
Nothingness
Offer infinite
Thoughts, ideas and
Dreams in the
Name of
"Discovery of the
Unknown"

That is the
Journey called,
"What an
Ephemeral
Splendor"

Where
Nothingness keeps
All that is;
Spinning forever...

Off the
Track

**Big minds
In search of
Truth via
Different routes:**

**Induction,
Deduction,
Causal inference or
The dialectics, but
No perfect clarity,
Yet**

**Big minds
Probed many
Possible ways, but
The result is still
The same**

**Even religions,
Mythical archetype
Unconscious and
Ideologies didn't
Meet the full
Expectations**

**Salute to the
Sublimed and
The damned for
Ignoring the moral
Being within...**

Intelligent
Being

Every
Intelligent
Being,

Breaths at
The cross road,
"What is right
And what is
Not?"

Every
Intelligent
Being,

Ready to
Explore,
"What is the
Meaning of it all"

Every
Intelligent
Being,

Seeks to lift
Above all the
Trivial noise…

To Rise
Above

Come,
Let us lit the
Light within

I mean,
Time to know,
"We're
Inseparable
Cosmic souls"

Let us
Be free from
Fragmenting
Forces:

Hate, violence,
And wars and
Relearn to be
At Peace

Let us
Rise above false
Narratives and
Myopic claims and
Be an awakened
Harmony, at last…

The Cage

Being,
What a
Cosmic vibration;
Humming in the
World of
Imperfection

Being,
What a big dream
Looking for truth
Before
He is no more

Being,
Always a shining
Star; bursting with
Mighty strength of
Impermanence

Being,
What a grand
Wheel keeps
Spinning, but never
Completing the
Cycle for himself...

Noble
Path

It's a
Direct mystical
Beginning

That's where
We're the
Meditative order
In the Universe

Oh yes,
That "Silent "is
A necessity to be
Free from sensory
Experience

Let us
Be the glowing
Spirits into this
*Anthrocosmic
Unity...*

Indefatigable

Though
Caught into
Constant storms,
We must remain
Steady on the trail

Though
The world is
Fragmented in
Many ways,

We
Must remain
Calm and alert
While pursuing
The mission called,
"Harmony"

Don't
Forget,
Each is
An unbroken
Wholeness
Blended by the
Moral fortitude;
So keep the bold
Journey on…

My
Journey

Beyond
What was and
What will is none
Of my concern
Until I is
A manifested,
"Truth" in the
Present

No point
In the state of
Guilt, grief
Or regret, if I've
To Grasp,
"What is the
Meaning of my
Core Essence"

Let
My courage
Blend with
Freewill and
And worthiness;
Before 'am
No more...

The
Issue

Wonder,
What if we are
The probability,
Uncertainty or just
An unpredictable
Experience to be

What if
We're to evolve
Beyond,
Where certainty
Is sovereign

If that is
True, in that
Case,
"What're we
Doing in this
Place?'

What
If we are still
Looking from a
Subjective notion
To grasp
The objective
Truth or what!

World
Today

Just delete
Greed, selfishness,
Vanity, envy and the
Rest and you're
Instantly a
Good human

That's been
The universal
Message, but
Ignored by the
Most

Not God, but
Human alone is
Responsible
Either to bring
Peace or war

It is from
Hungry rulers,
"Pious "servants
And dictators;
History is
Deeply blood-
Stained, always

Let's stop
This never
Ending insanity
And let's dare
To be the
Good humans…

The
Mission

God is
Indeed nameless
In reality, but we
Invented the term
To calm our fears of
The unknown

We
Pray Him daily
We worship Him
For our selfish need,
Simply

And that is
Why He is never
Near to our world
Of despair, violence
And wars

We got
To change the
Course of
Our collective
Thought and

Take
Responsibility to
Be a cooperative spirit;
Lifting humanity to the
Good end...

Cave
Dwellers

Funny,
We're born
Equal, but as
Grown-ups,
We're separated
By the fragmented
Ideologies and Beliefs

We waste
Time in thinking
Being better than
"Them" and
We constantly
Fight to impose
Our wills on others
To rule

As a
Consequence,
Many million deaths
And bloody wars
Wrote the sick
History of our kind

Let's teach
Children to begin
Their future with
New chapter of
Harmony and hope...

The
Task

Keep
Exploring Wisdom
For there is a dearth
Of it today

Keep
Strengthening
The moral force
For we've forgotten
Our way to the good

Let us
Not be disillusioned
And succumb to the
State of despair

Come,
Let us resurrect,
"Global Spirit of unity"
And let us roll forward
With a right purpose,
Today...

Our
Truth

No, we're
Not alone, but
We coexists here
And beyond

Yes, we're
Eternal sparks
In this everlasting,
"All That Is"

We're
Intelligent beings
We're born, we die
And come alive again
In this magnificent
Universe

"Forever" is the
Journey we've been
On since the beginning
And the beginning never
Comes to an end...

Casting
Shadows

Why this
Collective conscience
Been in
Slumber so long?

There are
Thunders of change
All over; sadly they
Have not woke-up
Yet

Oh this magic
Techno-addictions
And hedonistic life;
So fatal to the
Succeeding
Generations

Is it not
Time to open-up
All dimensions of
Good in such a stygian
Night!

Insidious

That lovely
Lady oh yes
She's so smart,

Yet
So tough, if
Things don't go
Her ways

She knows
She's the owner
Of immense beauty
And wit

Of course,
She adores the
High societal ranks
And big wealth

And, she
Enjoys teasing
Men, if
They're willing
To be her slaves

That's the
Lovely lady,
Be sure
To watch out for
Your dignity and
Well-being!

Hello
Creativity!

Living
In the
Purpose-driven
Realm is nothing,
But to fight million
Unknowns at the same
Time

Where
Challenges
Keep growing
By the minutes and
The journey keeps
Turning so steep

Indeed,
Living with the
Old divinely claims,
Stalls the mind from
Grasping truth in
Time

Is there
A new way
To awaken
New insight, new
Understanding and
A moral will to conquer
The riddle in an instant!

Reflection

What if,
"Self" is
The sum of
All known and
Unknowns in their
Vibrating modes
Forever

What if,
Being is
The guinea-pig
In the grand
Experiment;
Still fighting
For his freedom!

Wonder,
Where is the
Demarcation
Between being and his
Mystical essence in this
Chaotic experience

Does he
Knows his
Responsibility or not
Does he
Know his possibility?
Does he
Understand, "Who is he?"

Inflection

Not running
Away, but willing
To fulfill my moral
Call even if it takes
Too long

This life,
Only my chance
To make some
Difference while
Am on the highway
Of all my dreams

I must
Awake, arise and
Keep walking along
The rough track for
There is not much
Time left to debate

Yes,
I must be
A mighty force
Of determined will
And get ready to move
The mountain high

Let,
I gain my strength
From within and let
The rest be done with
Ease and calm from
This instant on...

Think
Future

There can't
Be a waiting
Game, but the
Ascension is the
Only course

There is
Neither I
Nor You,
But together
We're the
Riders of our
Mission

I mean,
We're the
Discovery of our
Noble Truth

Discard
The triviality of
Divided and
Falsified divinely
Notion and

Roll-up the
Sleeves and begin
The walk with
Heads-up toward,
Common destiny from
This moment on…

Boldness

In this
Boiling cauldron
Of grief and joy
We've
Been bobbing, dying
And revving over and
Again

First,
We got to shut
The fire of evil forces
And then jump off
The tribal container
As soon as we must

Let's
Lung into the
Cool stream
And let us swim
All the way to the
Ocean full of all
Possibilities and big
Dreams

Don't
Stand still and be
Fearful of the unknown
'Cause Unknown is
Our collective quest,
All the way to the
End…

Bloodline

We are
Offspring's of the
Historic struggles
That's been on for
Sometimes

Is it
Not time,
To rethink,
To reimaging and be
Creative for a change

I mean,
To ensure
Full essence of
Our genuine being
In this twenty-one!

Why
Don't we let go
Duality, "Good
And evil' and move on
With our purpose of
"Unity" simply...

Measure

What in the
World is this
Unique blend
Named, "Being"

Why is he
Fighting
To be "Good"
When
He already is

Why is he
Generous with
His materiality
And not so
With moral
Sense

Why is
He lost while
Knowing
The direction
So well!

Rubicon

Let's
Roll the dice
And see where it
Falls either here
Or beyond our
Thoughts

Let's
Revive the
Dead
"Global Spirit"
And be worthy
Of our births

It's a
Glorious sin
To keep reading
The bloody pages
Of history when
They never end

Why
Don't we get-
Off the cage and
Be the intelligent
Beings, we've
Been since the
Beginning!

Get Off

Let
Fragile hope
Blossom soon or
We'll be
Bobbing into the
State of despair for
A long

Let
Guardians
Come to their
Common-senses and
Show the way to
Goodness and unity
As the norm

Let religious
Zealots get off the
Highway of
Death and
Destruction and
Allow
Humanity to
Rise above all...

Jeopardy

Is it
All about
Self identity or
Something more
To think of

Is it
The concern
About freedom
Or what

How
Do we kill:
Alienation,
Fear and despair

When
Many million
Young are dying
From drugs, wars,
Violence's and much
More...

Becoming

Value
Judgments
Directing human
Behavior through
The timelessness of
All that we know

They propel
Him to live well
With some meaning

Indeed,
The value
Judgments being
Driving force; leading
Him to know his role

In the end,
It's the power of
Value judgments
That determines
Our collective path,
"Who we are and
What we ought to be."

Mystical
Bliss

What if,
"I" is the moral
Being, *de jure*

In
That case,
Will "I"
Roll from
Temporal to
Eternal or what!

What if,
"I" is a
Pure abstraction,
Will it awaken my
Metaphysical soul,
Or not!

Why
"I" is thrown
Into this turmoil:
Bigotry, violence
And insanity
For what

How long
Before "I" is
Freed from this
Diseased
Human being!

Magic
Ride

I
Can't say
Face to face
My lady, but
Only through
These few words,
I shall sing our
Immortal song:

It's been a
Morning since
Love found us
Eons ago

It's been
Truth kept
Us inseparable
Since we took
The solemn vows

What a
Magic ride,
To be in love
With you, indeed

Global
Anthem

Let
Children play
And be happy
While they got the
Time

Let
Young be free
But learn to be
Responsible from
The very beginning

Let
Grown-ups
Act morally to
Inspire young
To be good

Let
Leaders
Learn to govern
The ship with
Tolerance and
Inclusion

Let
Humanity be the
"Global Spirit"
Powered by
Unity, peace and
Understanding...

Miracle
May not

Standing
Alone in this
Vastness of
The unknown;

Trying
So hard to
Comprehend
The glowing
Reality in full

Imagine,
Only handful
Spirits won the
Game, but
Billions
Still waiting
In the wing

The path is
Open to all,
Why then
A few made it
All the way to
Their own Truth!

Voyagers

Dear Girl,
Only through
Your love,
I've known
The meaning of
Our essence

Your
Smile has been
My strength

Your
Sacrifices been
My success

Your
Inspiration;
Never a separation
Between dream
And
Reality, at all

Glad
We've been,
"Two into One"
All along through
The mighty
Rough Sea...

Resilience

Well
Life is
Short and the
Journey so long.
In such a
Reality, at times
Existence seems
Impossible

And in such
Milieu,
We end-up
Losing identity,
Our mission and
The joy of being
Human

Time
To relearn,
"How to quiet
Anxiety and get off
The feeling of being
Forlorn"

Let us
Remain Silent
And introspect the
Strength within and

Think,
We're the
Masters and
Not tear droppers,
At all…

Cosmic
Being

Perhaps
All these obstacles
Are here to clarify,
"What is my truth?"

That's why,
I must
View reality
From the eye of
Eternity from this
Moment on

What if,
Paradoxically,
I am truth and
Still lost in the
Riddle of it all?

Let
The inner spirit
Awaken and let the
Meaning be grasped
While I am riding
Through my brief
Time...

The
Call

"Self
Renewal"
That is the
Golden key to
Remember

That is
The habit,
To go after

Let
There be
A constant
Zeal to fly off
The edge

Let I
Seize
The moment,

Let I
Dust off
Darkness and
Clear the way...

It's
Time

Cooperative
Spirit is the final
Act to save humanity
And the planet itself

That's why,
Moral courage
With
Rational insight
Must be the
Force behind

Dated
False narratives
Of yesterday be
Dropped in this
Age of
New beginning

Tribal claims
Of Divinity too is
No longer valid
In this Twenty-One

Time to
Adapt to new
Reality of human
Survival and to save
Future of the offspring's...

Images

What if,
We're
The images
Of this dying
Universe!

What if,
There is no
Escape from
The big bubble

How long
Do we keep?
Ignoring our fate
Into such a dark
Place

Will that
Mean,
We shall never
See our images into
The mirror of this
Dying universe,
Or what!

Roaring
Fans

Damn right,
We're the
Winners no
Matter what
May be the
Consequence

Damn right,
We're here
To win
The game and
We,ll fight to
The end

We
Don't care
What happens
To the otherside,
All we want is to
Win the game

Damn right,
That's our
Stubborn pledge
And nothing more
But to win the game,
In th end, alright...

Rose

Oh that
Rose, how
Gracefully
Flowing through
The stream;
Carrying all
My dreams

A stream,
That is
Meandering
Through the
Rough terrain
Now and then

Many
Thunders and
Lightenings kept
Threatening
Its fate, but the
Rose keeps
Rolling with
Full calm

What a
Magic is that
Beauty and truth;
Heading towards
The Blue Sea...

Forever

Hey Gal,
What
Happened
To your
Sweet words,
When
We met the
First time

Hey Gal,
Where is your
Sweet smile
When we
Fell in love the
First time

Was that
Just a dream,
Or just one
Big joke ;
Wounding my
Ego or what

Hey Gal,
Quit the game
And be mine for
I am in love with
You forever...

**Free
Flow**

**Pledge for
What?
When we've
Just arrived
To discover our
Truth**

**That's been
The moral mission
We intended to meet
As free spirits**

**Why keep
Hiding under His
Name and not be
An independent beings;
Defining our common
Destiny at this time**

**Why keep
Apologzing
Every time, when
We're the fearless
Born to seek our
Solemn Truth...**

With or
Without

Caught
Into this conflict
Zone of fragmented
Beliefs

Where
I struggle to be
Happy, but the
Contradictions is
The issue

To be tackled
Before launching
My journey to the,
"Self-meaning"

In this
Total Reality,
Not easy to carry on
Reason and moral
Courage consistently

Especially, when the
World is succcumbed
To His Big Name,
Already …

Sacred
Mission

What is
This world when
"Intelligent inhabitants,"
Fail to grasp the simple
Truth

What is
This journey when
No directions are
Posted along the
Highway of violence
Ans war

I ask
Why are we
Unable to define
A right connectivity
In our relationships

Come,
Let us adapt and
Learn how to walk along
The Spirit of Oneness...

Consequence

While
Hanging in this
Nothingness called,
"Existence"and no
Place to go, but fly off
From the unknown edge

Either we
Emerge with
Hellish attitude or we
Ascend to the
Heavenly inspiration

That is
The choice, and
That is the freedom,
But either ways;
Consequences be
Paid in time

Let us
Make a right move
With new attitude and
Be in Harmony,
At every turning point
Of life and time,
What we own them
For a brief…

Our
Time

When
There is nothing
Left, but sheer ignorance,
We cease to be humans

All we get
In return, perhaps,
"Twenty-first century
Scenario in-making!"

Look at,
Climate is threatening
More frequently than
Ever

A few mad-men
Are ready to blow-up
The world in a minute

There is a growing
Bitter attitude toward
One another and

There is an
Emerging insanity;
Killing very goodwill
Of the inner being, but
The world still in its
Deep slumber!

Big
Stride

Needs bit of a
Minor adjustment:

Let moral will
Be the divinely
Freedom of human
Beings

Let them
Be free to define
Their genuine meaning
Of existence

Letthem
Sail through the
Crises of their making

And let them resolve
With the power of
Reason and vision

Letthem
Endeavor and
Connect with their
Enlightened Spirits

Let humans
Be independent of
All imposed constraints
And be returned to
Theira uthenticity,
At once…

Enigma

We're
Born under the
Canopy of million
Riddles to face and
 seem there is never
An end

That is
Our beginning
And that shall be
Always the
New beginning,

We're
Dancing with
Milion dreams
With contesting
Wills;

Ending
In duality: Hope and
Despair, grief and joy
And many more

We're
The accidental
Invention and got
No clue, "Where
Is the right direction
To roll..."

Awakening

Enough
Of all our
Glorious
Bblunders

Time
To move on;
Strengthening
The world of
New ideas and
New vision

No point
Standing still
In the state of
Suffering and
Being forlorn

Let's
Come together;
Lifting the spirit
Higher than ever
And be the winners,
That we must...

Renewal

Each
Beautiful
Morning
Is the best gift
Where am into
The full-Silence

Where
Nothing, but
The soft breeze;
Running through
My spirit

As the Sun
Ascends so do my
Intutive inspiration

And,
By the time,
It sinks beneath
Horizon, I am not
In that experience

Glad, there is
Always another
Beautiful morning;
Shining my soul
With every breath
Of moral spirit...

Profile

Being,
What a growth
And change,
Always in-making

Being,
A continuum
Force;
Marching with
Others to meet the
Set dream

Being,
What a
Spontenous
Mystical courage;
Williing to share
His common destiny,
Others like him

Being,
What an eternal
In action;
Searching for his
Only Truth...

Continuum

It used be
A long talk at
The dinner table,
But lately it's a
Rare experience

In the old
Days, time was
Left to interact
Face to face

Landing
In the present,
We're tied up,
Virtually with
Our techno-toys
24/7

After
Briefly wishing
Well over the
Phone,

We hung up,
For "No Time" left,
But to serve the old
Techno old habit…

Rebirth

Being,
Always a
Wonderous
Child of the
Cosmic seed

Let him
Gains his
Self-confidence

And
Know the
Authentic
Worthiness
From the very
Start

Let him
Evolve soon
To drop: ignorance,
Arrogance and
Indifferent attitude,
For the first time...

Will to
Win

No more
An utopian adventure
And no more a chimerical
Notion to kick around

There is
No sense holding onto
The old wishes and
Dreams, if there is no
Peace and harmony,
Left in the game

Time
To get off
The track of
Jingoistic obsession
Time to
Gear-up to be the
Pragmatic best...

Loving
You

Loving you
Is real to be
Human again

Loving you
Is the only way
To walk
Through life

Yes, darling
Loving you
Is the
Only solemn
Journey to me

Yes,
Sweet Heart,
Loving you
Is the truth, I've
Only known ...

Fortitude

Keep
Running 'til
The path leads
You to your
Ultimate Good

Leap forward
With freewill
'Til You've seized
The essence at the
Core

Don't be
Shy and don't
Run away from the
Challenge on-hand

Keep faith
In the self and keep
Knocking the door
Until you've unleashed
Your will to win...

Get-up
& Go

I shall
Never give-up
The mission,
I've
Been on for
A long

I shall
Attain the
Victory of
My time

Let each
Soul sing his
Immortal song

Each has
To join the march
To save the Mother
Earth and ourselves
Before neither
May be!

Salute

In this
Magnificent silence
Of all that is

Let the
World awake with
Goodwill each morning

Human,
What a thunder bolt
Of million possibilities

Human
What a moral glow
Dare

To walk through
The narrow tunnel of
Darkness and be the
Light himself...

Pursuit

Where
Mind and matter
Are one

Where
Subject and object
Don't differentiate,
Any more

That is
How the inner
Identity of each
Being be defined

That is
Where reality be
Grasped in an
Instant

That is
The path to be
Explored and

That is
How, the holistic link
Between the Self and
The Mighty Universe,
Be spontenously
Undertood…

Transdence

Seems,
We're the only
Mirror of our
Constant curiosities,
Geared to unfold the
Truth; whatever it
May be

We're
The illuminations
Willing to take a
Bold step,
Yes,
To resolve the mystery
On-hand

No need to
Be divine and no
Need to be arrogant

Simply,
Be sincere to
Attain the mission,
On time...

That
 # Is It

This birth is
A challenge to
Attain my dream

Whatever
Time I've is
The only best gift
That I must cherish
It well

I've no
Time either to grief
Or be in despair

I've
Only few moments to
Spare all the way
To my truth

Indeed,
I know, "There is
Neither hell nor
Heaven, but the
Death is certain."

Long
Walk

**There is
A meaning between
Human purpose and
His waiting destiny,
*Substratum***

**That is
Why, he is
Passing through
Many trials and
Tripeditions**

**Let him
Walk along the
Tough terrain and**

**Let him
Measure, the depth
 Of his commitment…**

Truth
As Is

Unbroken
Wholeness known
Via "nonlocal" reality
Is the confirmation of
Brahman indeed

Holographic
Projection is
The fact; verifying
Such a metaphysical
Entity as well

 It's always,
The reality spinning
Around the permanence,
 "Brahman"

Bubbles of
Universe, life, death
 and rebirth
Keep popping-up in
The impermanence,
Yet, the enigma
Remains always…

Eternal
Dance

Birth and
Death,
What a
Romantic dance
Of life forever

Being
What a magic,
" Who is always
Something"

Life and
Death, what an
Endless drama,
Yet so brief

Life and
Death,
What a thread
Line to be the asset
To the world

Birth and
Death,
What a beautiful
Dance with a purpose…

Reality
As Is

What if
Reality stands,
As is without
A First cause

I mean,
When its
Powered by the
Deep Silence of
The human mind only!

Reality
Perhaps a magic,
"Self-transformation"
Without an external
Agency; climbing
The hidden dream

Reality,
Always a realm of
Constant creativity,
Connectivity and
Rational perfection…

Mystical
"I"

"I" just
A correlation
Between natural
Events and human
Affairs simply

"I" perhaps
A living symbol
Of life that is
So brief, but quite
Challening

Who knows,
What this "I"
Means in this
Many dimensional
Chaotic riddles

"I" just a
Victim of greed,
Lies and false
Narratives

Let "I"
Escape from
It all and
Return to the
Source…

Enlightenment

Bhagvad-Gita
The celestial song
Echoing the basic
Message of moral
Boldness

It's an
Open ethical
Guide;

Calling each
To be the
Conqueror of the
Mind

It asks to
Perform your
Duty and
To let truth
Prevail over greed,
Lies and deceptions…

Challenge

Integrity of the
Will is the biggest
Challenge to keep
The jounrey steady

That being
The essence of this
Struggling existence

Don't let
The human condition,
Obscure the value
To be a genuine being

And don't let
Bickerings disturbed
The intended noble goal...

Arrow
In Flight

Spinning
Arrow in flight
Nobody knows
Where will it hit the
Target in the dying
Universe

Spinning
Thoughts flying
Off the wondering
Human mind,

When are
They going to
Knock off the
Hidden riddles of
His truth

All is
In silence;
Spinning quietly,
From one generation
To another and
No answer yet!

Melody

Dear Love,
What a wonder
You've sparked
In my world

Love,
Yes my dear
You've turned
Dream into every
Song of joy

Love,
Yes my soul
You've given
Melody to our
Romance

Love,
Let's celebrate
Life and
Salute this beautiful
Experience,

We've been
In since our every
Beginning over and
Again…

Confession

Sometimes
I laugh and
Sometimes I
Don't

Sometimes,
I am on the
Track and
Sometimes am
Not

Sometimes
I walk through
The light and
Sometimes, I am
Lost in the dark

But
No matter,
I am always in
Love with you,
Dear heart

Yes,
I confess,
"Am lost in the
Dream of your
Love, your love...
Your love, forever..."

Verdict

Yes, we
Wrote the history
Half n'half with
Million mischiefs,
Lies and greed

Is it
Not time to
Flip the trend
And begin new
Pages with good
Intent!

Many
Thousand
Years passed by
And human nature
Hasn't changed

How
Long this finite
Semi-evolved being
Shall withstand,
Old bad habits of the
Mind...

Note ,
Well

Every hour,
Every minute and
Every sec

We're in
Renedezous with
Death

That is
The shadow lurking
Since our births and

That is
The way journey
Rolls on
'Til we're no
More on the scene

Knowing
This truth, let's
Just complete the
Solemn mission
As soon as we must...

Introspection

Being
Alone is in
Contest with his will;
Resulting in duality:
Hope and despair,
Grief and joy and
Many more

Being,
Alone seems
An accidental
Invention of nature;
Willing to save and
Destroy her at the
Same time

Being,
Judges his validity
Via narccissitic ways
While his humanity,
Hangs in the realm
Of uncertainty,
Alright!

Will
To Roll

Did you
Learn,
Human is never
A shadow but an
Eternal Spark in
Universe!

Did you
Know,
Human not a
Miserable experience,
But an eternal hope

If you
Do identify
Your inner being
With such a simple
Truth

Are you
Willing to leap
Forward powered by
Your indomitable
Will to win!

Being & Mission

Our
Linguistic strength
Arises from good
Thoughts, words and
Ideas we express
Before the world

Yes, they're
The base references
To be in relationship
With many billion
Others

Our
Essence is the
Power; ensuring
Ascension to the
Meaning and melody,

What
We wish to explore
And to understand

That is the
Primary step to
Make it through
While on a linguistic
Journey of clarity alright…

**Empty
Theater**

And now
The curtain
Is open to end
The affair

We shared
Life together
For a while

Yes,
We'd our
Facinations
And faults while
Dancing through
Our time

But, then
We're humans;
Blended by our
Imperfections;

Throwing us
Into the theater
Of the absured and
Now asking to bid,
"Goodbye…"

Overture:
21st

Why in the
Name of this
"Solemn Silence"
I must rock this
Ship

Why go
Through the
Struggle to look
For my meaning

When the
World is heading
Toward the dark

Let
The Light within
Leads "Every I"
To get off the blured
Vision…

Die
Hard

Where all
Is in flux and
Still steady through
The time

That is
The state of
Human nature,
And history is
Written in that
Set format

That's the
Reality of humans,
Who keeps evolving
Half-n-half

Through
Trials & Errors of
Existence

That's the
Dilemma of human
Essence; struggling
Forever to perfect
Himself…

Pretenders

We
Keep knocking
The Temple doors
To enter the sanctum
Every time

Yet we fail
To grasp the deep
Meaning, "What is
Our Truh?"

That's the
Blatant sin we
Ignore and continue
To go on living while
Here for a brief…

Noble
Souls

Folks
To whom
I adored, already
Left the scene
Sometime ago

What a
Flash of time
While journeying
With "em all

Though
Existence a constant
Struggle, they enriched
My worthiness
Yes, at every
Step of the walk with
Them

Oh yes,
They we're all
Noble souls of
Love, respect and
Courage

Life, even
So full of twists and
Turns, it was still a
Divine journey with
Them all…

Force
Majeure

When
Walking along
The trail of
Moral action,

Divinity
Must be the truth of
Such noble souls

 Remember.
Awakened
Beings,

Always a
Moving force of
Positive change and
Growth

They are
Inspirations and
The world is saved
From full destruction,
Every time

Let us
Emulate their
Inner strengths and
Let us begin the walk
Along their inspired path
From this moment on...

Naked &
Damned

What if
We are the living
Nothing?

I mean,
What if we are
Evolving towards
Death only!

When
Human is
Separated from
His core principle,

Is not
Just another
Hedonistic worm
Living off his greed

Wonder,
Where else can he
Hide in this twenty-one?"

The
Quest

Let's
Relearn,
 "How to
Give a damn"

 Being,
Hanging in the
Sphere of anxiety
And uncertainty

Yes,
It's the serious
Issue called,
 "Either live or die"

I mean,
What if the future of
Children; twisting
In thin air…

Nothingness

When
I drop dead,
All that is here
Shall be nothing in
An instant

If lucky,
A few will tear
For a while

Then I shall
Be just another
Fading memory
In time

Perhaps,
My image will
Be hanging in a
Photo frame and

It too
Shall lost forever
In distance time...

Flyover

Let's
Just fly over
This serrated
Terrain and

Be
The freewills and
Reach the distance
Reality to know
Our Truth

Why waste
Time in the world
Of vanity, envy and
Greed

Why not
Humanity fly off
To eternity and rest
In peace…

Being &
Meaning

Truth is
Our logical
Necessity and

That's how
I learn to
Resolvemy worth,
Sensu strictu

Indeed,
My quest is
Essential to unfold
Reality with full-
Clarity

I, an existence
Without essence
Means am living
In the state of
Perpetual illusion

And
That is not
Acceptable while
Am walking along
The unknown trail;
Leading me to the truth…

Infidelity

Please,
Don't you
Hurt family for
Your concupiscence
Adventures

Damn right,
When you cheat
Other- half.... you
Shatter her dreams
Forever

 You break
Her total humanity
That never heals
In time

Please,
Don't be slave to
The old habit

For its
A deep emotive blow
To the other-half and
 The kids...

Cause &
Consequence

A child lost
On the land where
Drought and despair
Governed his fate

That child
Lost mom and pop
In starvation; leaving
At the mercy of the
Unfriendly world

With nothing to
Grow-up but poverty
And hunger, all
Biting the soul,

Slowly he
Begins to hate the
World and turns an easy
Prey to the nemesis
Of Good

Once an innocent
Helpless, soon begins
To kill many with
No remorse

Well, the world fails
To save many like him
As their number
Grows…so the story of
Human tragedy beats on...

Disconnectivity

Well off
Consumers
Enjoying their
Material toys

Do they know,
There is a hefty
Price to be paid,
In return

Yes, it's the
Pressing issue of
The "Climate refugees"
Heading north in big
Numbers

Yes, it's the
Challenging influx
Of millions from the
War torn zones and
Many failed states

That is
The consequence
Of a myopic blueprint
Backed by ignorance,
Arrogance and too much
Greed ever exploiting…
 "Have nots of the world."

Holitic
Reality

While being
Deep in the state of
Efflorcent bliss,

Clarity of my
Vision emerges,
Spontenously each
Time

Its a
Wonderful magic
Joining "I" with
The natural patterns
Of the universe, or
What!

Seems,
"I" the Soul is the
"Holistic unity"
As always

 "I" the
Recepient of whatever
Truth, keeps nearing
 To it, each time!

Being
It Is

Wonder,
Why keep hanging
Aimelessly between
Half-Truth and half-Lie

Why not seek
An easy passage
To be a freewil and
Transcend to the
World of Good

Why keep
Begging to be
Good when we're
The masters of
It all

Let's leave
The world of
Fragmented beliefs,
Idealogies and the
State of darkness and
Declare ourselves to be
"Free forever…"

Wake-up
Call

The world is
On fire and
Dying slowly
Through the
Time

Do we have a
Right willingness
To extinguish it,
Or not?

The world is
Plagued by the
Wonton wars

As many
Millions displaced
From their homelands
And many yet to die

All major
Players are playing
Their silent games

Whilest the
Common folks are
Paying a deadly
Prize…

Excelsior

Time
To focus on
Nurturing the
Global Spirit,
"Wholeness"

 Time
To be free
From the evil
Habits now

Time
To give a damn
And save humanity
And the Planet itself

Time
To awaken the
Inner being and
The moral sense

Yes, to save
Future of children
Through right actions
And not sweet talks...

Courage,
Exclusively

Only in
Harmony,
There is sovereign
Happiness of all

That is
The best experience
To attened while
The ride is on

That is the
Way we shall
Emerge to be the
Enlightened humans,
Time after time

Let's then
Get on the right
Track and reach the
Noble mission so set...

Point
Upward

Only
Through
Self-realization,
We shall lit a new
Reality, "Being
 Becoming,"at last

Only through
Awareness,
"Anthrocosmic
 Unity," we've
Chance to go
Beyond

Let us
Begin to know,
Our supreme
Pssibilities and

Reemerge
Being the moral
Force of change...

Ripples

Everything
Is a hidden reality
Working beneath the
Meandering stream

It's from
Liitle things
Life evolves into a
Giant meaning on
It's own

It's from
Tiny event,
There emerges,
The essence of
Everybeing on
The roll

It's from
The invisible
Soul, moral boldness
Goes into action and

Intelligent beings,
Transforming from
Nothing into something
Called, "Self-awakening."

Action

What is our
Base reference
From where
We can
Fly-off to the
Realm of beauty
And truth

Where is
The blue-print
Taking us to the
World of sanity and
Dignity at once

Who's
To guide us to the
Highest peak of
Goodwill and unity,
But our collective
Endeavor

Let us
Commit to
Understanding
And cooperative
Spirit to take care of
 Our well-being…

Godly
Freedom

Let God,
Be free from the
False narratives
And dogmatic claims

Let Him
Be the individual's
Moral inspiration;
Driving him toward
His set goal

Let God
Be the force of
Goodwill in every
Huma; bringing
Harmomy to the
Whole

Let's
Get busy with
Godly mission called,
"Self-endeavor to build
A better world"

Copyright © 2022 by J.J. Bhatt

That's
Him

No need
To be dogmatic
Of your belief

No need
To claim Him
As if you're the
Owner

No need to kill
Others in His name

He's an
Open truth equal
In every respect to
All

He's
Merciful and
Equal justice
To all

For Him,
Its His One family
Called, "Humanity,"
That's all...

Inner
Being

While
On the assembly
Line between the
Beginning and end

The Soul,
Is the only
Proppeling force
In the universe

Soul,
Yes this creative
Awakening light;
Streches from known
Toward the unknown
Forever

Soul,
Yes this engimatic
Spirit; heading north
Toward the very truth
Of all…

Trust

Darling,
There is
No distance
Between our
Feelings today

There is
No excuse to
Avoid each other
Between now and
Eternity

Yes,
Dear babe,
We're in love and
There must be
 no words in-between

Let, the
 "Silent Trust" be
The only thread; saving
 Our souls forever, forever...
Forever…

Off the
Slumber

When
Intelligent beings
Are driven by good
Thoughts

Why
Haven'tthey
Conquored the
Evil consequences
Of history, thus far

Even when
Listening to the
Wisdom of great
Minds

Why then
They' ve been
Rotting into the
Dark side!

What is the
Source oftheir
Demise that they
Can't even identify,
"Who they are?"

Why
Tolerate living
In this world of
Insecurity, fear and
Despair?

Integrity

It's time,
To let go bad
Memories and
Trivial things

It's time
To rethink and
Begin a new path
Full of hope

It's the
Humanalone;
Defining the world
Either right or
Wrong

Each human
Action too shapes
The world either
Good or bad

Let's
Continue the
Journey along a
Highway called,
Intgrity of the mind

And be the
Winners in
This challenging
Time...

We
Exists

There is
A bright glow
In every being
It's called,
 "Conscience"

There is
A strong force
Of good in
Every child we see
Them at play

There is
An impressive
Vigor in young
Braves,

But they've
Succumbed to bad
Habits of their
Time

There is
A good intention
In many grown-ups,
But lack the
Necesssary moral
Courage to prove it
In action...

Great
Wheel

Being though
An ephemeral
Splendor still
Dancing in the
Sphere of uncertainty
And fear

Being,
 Keeps searching;
"What is here for
Him?" and there is
No answer yet

What if,
He is a spinning
Impermanence
Wrapped around
The big wheel of
Permanence

What if
In this holographic
Reality, he is nothing,
But a mere projection!

Dear
Heart

Don't run
Away for
We've been in
Love since our
First dream

Don't
Be afraid and
Don't stand still for
We've been *one-soul*
Since the beginning

Dear heart,
Know well,
 "We've been
In love since first
Starlight awakened
Our spirits while
The world was asleep"

 I say
Dear heart,
"Gather-up your
Courage and return
To the world, *la amore*"
And be my forever...

Pivot

Is it true,
We're being reduced
Into numbers, categories
And codified without
Names or whatever
We don't understand

Do we ever
Ask, "What happened
To our good names, dignity
And our humanity that we
Thought had them forever"

And what about
These growing numbers
Of smart thinking robots,
We've been ignoring them
For sometime

Do we ever
Realize, now they are
Threatening our freedom,
I mean, they're
Already began to control
Our thoughts

Wonder,
What if we're
On a lost raft that is
Floating aimlessly around
The turbulent Techno-Sea!

How
Long!

How long
Should we ride in
The age of techno-
Opium world

How long
Humans should wait,
To save their humanity
While walking along
The techno-trail

And into this
Realm of violence
And wars, how long
Humans should wait
Before they lose their
Real identity

And how long
To be tolerated
To this reality of lies,
Deceptions and greed
Before children's dream
Shuld be saved?

Lost on A Trail

It's been a
Long journey
Of thousand years,
And there is never
A new beginning of
His human nature

Why
This dilemma
To face time after
Time,
When he is
Die Imago and
Power to change
The course

 Yet it's a
Long struggle
Of thousand years
And the end seems
Always too far...

Long
Walk

A journey
To be believed,
Before
Taking the first
Step

A choice
To be made,
Before
Rolling along
The road to the
Unknown

Yes, life be
Understood,
Before climbing
The tall mount

Let the
Jounrney be
Shortened with
Courage and
Freewill...

Being &
Essence

To grasp
All that is necessary
With the Silent
State of the mind

Yes, to know
The Self well
Before heading to
The mountain so
Very high

To become
A rational being
To build a right
Blueprint and

Learn,
"How to proceed
Against all odds"
Damn right,
Let it be the essence
 Of my "Witnessing
Consciousness"

Dimentia

It's been
An eternal battle
Between good and
Evil that we know
So well

It's been
A life driven by
"trials and errors,"
Alright

We're
Intelligent beings
Who're lost into
Stubborn ignorance
And violent attitude

 Recall,
We've arrived
To the twenty-first
After many wars
Of the twenteith

And still
We keep bobbing
Into this milieu of
Anxiety, fear and
Uncertainty as ever...

Prayer

Dear Lady
Destiny, when
Will you give us
The key to open
The doors to your
Ultimate beauty

Dear Lady
Destiny, when
Shall we enter the
Sanctum of the
Real meaning and
Be the part of your
Eternity

Dear Lady,
Destiny, just inspire
Us, " Howto turn
This divided humanity
Into one mighty unity."

The
Scenario

It's the
Reality today
Where uncertainty
Spins every where

Every being
So alive feels unable
To nmake a difference
For whatever reason

Meanwhile,
He is overwhelmed
By the rapid changes
And feels forlorn
At every step of
The way

Guardians
Failing to correct the
Human condition and
Unable to check violence
And myopic beliefs;
Undermining humanity's
Strength…

Mystical
Will

This
Wonderful magic
Of being alive must
Be appreciated always

This
Eternal spark
Called, "Human"is
The most precious
Gift ever

This
Evergreen beauty
Of the Planet Blue is
Seranading every
Time for sure

We're here
To take us to the
Dominion of Perfection

Let us
Believe and keep
The bold journey rolling ...

Inner
Being

Every mystery
Revolves within
The being himself

As he piles up
The petite mind
With million queries,
In return

His Soul,
What an enigmatic
Cosmic intrigue and
An Unspoken Will

Yes, the Soul,
What a magical form
Pressed onto the
Human substance with
A noble purpose

Soul,
Where Good prevails
And where a constant
Flow of light keeps
Flashing as ever...

Persevers

Many
Paradign shifts
Have come and
Gone and still to
Come

For the
Giant leap of the
Curious mind is
The source of it all

That is
The story. That is the
Glory. That is the
Journey of the human
Spirit still on

It's the
Creative thoughts.
It's the power of
Imaginations. It's
The boldness and
Genius of the being
Himself; keepng
Hope alive...

Let's
Rise

Is it not
Time to ascend
To the highest peak
And view the world
From eternity's eye!

That is the
Challenge. That is
The tease. That is
The nut to be cracked.

Is it not
Time to be bold
And arise from the
Long slumber and
Be the awakened spirits
Of our collective worth

That is
The effort. That is
The direction. That is
The necessary confidence
Be emanated from every
Soul...

Apercu

"I," what a
Tiny speck floating
Within all whims

Yes,
"I" still
Lost, not knowing
Essence so well

"I,"
Just another
Ego dancing for a
Brief

"I,"
What a mirror
Of humanity,
Driven by ambitions
And dreams

Let "I" be
The turning point,
And let the story roll
Forward in his time…

\\

Redressing

What if
This half-baked
Mental pie is
Nothing but acopy
Cat

Its a madness,
Chasing the old
Symbols with new
Lables

Most mystical
Insights have been
Redressed with new
Garments, but
Truth remains the
Same, *substratum*

Notion of
Multiverses, eleven
Dimensions, eternal
Existence and so-called
"Implicate and explicate
Orders" are but the
Echoes from the deep
Vedic essence…

This Age
of Info!

To evicerate
All false
Preachings that
Promote violence
And war

To reject
Fake news;
Trying to control
Our thoughts

 To learn,
"How to discern
Truth in-between
The blured lines"

To be
Calm and alert;
How to navigate
Through the cess
Pool of the time

What a
Fate to be living
In this age of mass
 Misinformation?

All for What?

Have we
Ever thought,
We're continuum
Consciousness free

Have we ever
Noted, we're the
Temporals in flight
Toward Eternals

Let it beknown:
Each is an ascending
"Self," and
Being free from
Life and death

Indeed, we're
Fleeting events
With or without
A meaning, and
There is
No need to apologies
Any time soon…

Beware!

Let our
Collective spirits
Be the mighty
Wave-makers

Let the
World keep running
On the moral track,
Yes to stop the tide of
Unacceptable change

Our world is so
Over charged with
Their lies, deceptions
And sibbolths, let it
All turn into,
"Nothing whatsoever"

 Time to get
Smart and learn
To take charge and
Remove, "Who ever is the
Real culprit in the game."

Dust
Storm

While
Walking through
The harsh
Dry terrain,
We're lost into
The blinding dust
Storm

Our vision
Isn't as good as
It used to be

Our thoughts
Not as sharp
As they were
Once before

And, there is a
Loss of moral vigor
That we once used
To own,

I mean,
With full
 Pride and dignity,
At all time…

We
Shall

Let
Every thought
Lead us to a
Right action

Let
Every being
Be aware of the
Meaning of his
Journey

Human,
Alone is the
Real pearl; expanding,
 The sphere of many
Unknowns

 Let his
Core Essence
Be larger than
Life itself!

Veracity

In this
Mysterious
Reality of all that is,
"I" just a fearless
"Being Becoming"

That is
The purpose-driven
Trail to be understood
Well at each step of the
Way

"I" neither life nor
Death, but a cosmic
Essence evolving toward
Its ultimate perfection…

Perspicacious

It's
A simple
Purpose to be
Born human,

"To awaken
The Self and to
Perish evil in the
Mind"

Nothing
So abstruse and
Nothing so fancy
Just to grasp such
An simple,Truth

Let the
Purified mind,
Secure global
Cooperation;
Saving humankind
And the Planet itself."

Evolving
Spirit

When born,
There is a
Zero awareness
In that fragile
Human mind

When grown,
There is a bit more
Awarenes, but not so
Complete yet

Well in time
Awareness
Grows faster
When battered
By the mighty
Storms of existence

If he is smart,
He can dissovle
Dream into reality;
Conquoring the mind,
Itself ...

Cosmic
Breath

Our names
Are just labels
Given by someone else
Without our consent

Our individual
Journey is nothing,
But the choiceless
Path

At times,
We feel empty
And despair making
Us "Existentialists,"
At least, for a brief

No matter
What may be the
Conequence,
Our inner
 Being must never
Quit the confidence
And hope…

Magic
It Is

Every child
Born is a master
Of his/her universe,
Always

Every cry is
An expression of
Potentiality ready
To be unleashed

Let every
Child learn,
"How to nourish
His/her beginning
With a renewed spirit"

Every child
What a beautiful
Future; shining with
Sp many dreams

Every child
Born, what a real
Magic of tomorrow,
In full sense of human
Truth...

Consequential

Silence,
Balancing moral
And immoral at
The same time

His Soul;
Waiting to be
Fully awakened
To eliminate
Darkness from the
Scene

Such is
The state of
"I"
And there is no
Escape 'til knowing
The inner will

That is
The fragililty,
Being human and

That is
The unwritten
Inscription…

JAGDISH J. BHATT, PhD
Brings 45 years of academic experience
including a post- doctorate research
scientist at Stanford University, CA. He
holds an impressive authorship of over 50
books.